THE SIBLING SURVIVAL GUIDE

also by Dawn Huebner

Outsmarting Worry
An Older Kid's Guide to Managing Anxiety
Illustrated by Kara McHale
ISBN 978 1 78592 782 9
eISBN 978 1 78450 702 2

Something Bad Happened
A Kid's Guide to Coping With Events in the News
Illustrated by Kara McHale
ISBN 978 1 78775 074 6
eISBN 978 1 78775 075 3

THE SIBLING SURVIVAL GUIDE

SUREFIRE WAYS TO SOLVE CONFLICTS,
REDUCE RIVALRY, AND HAVE MORE FUN WITH
YOUR BROTHERS AND SISTERS

DAWN HUEBNER, PHD

ILLUSTRATED BY KARA MCHALE

Jessica Kingsley Publishers
London and Philadelphia

First published in Great Britain in 2021 by Jessica Kingsley Publishers
An Hachette Company

1

Copyright © Dawn Huebner 2021
Illustrations copyright © Kara McHale 2021

A CIP catalogue record for this title is available from the British
Library and the Library of Congress

ISBN 978 1 78775 491 1
eISBN 978 1 78775 492 8

Printed and bound in the United States
by West Publishing Corporation

Jessica Kingsley Publishers' policy is to use papers that are natural,
renewable, and recyclable products and made from wood grown
in sustainable forests. The logging and manufacturing processes
are expected to conform to the environmental regulations of the
country of origin.

Jessica Kingsley Publishers
Carmelite House
50 Victoria Embankment
London EC4Y 0DZ

www.jkp.com

Contents

A Note to Parents and Caregivers

There are few things more draining to parents than their constantly bickering children.

He's lying!

She went first last time!

He touched me!

She started it!

Why can't they just get along? It's a good question. One you've probably asked many times—perhaps in a voice several decibels louder than you'd care to admit.

Believe it or not, your children are not fighting to

torture you. Quite the opposite: they are trying to win your favor. Children are biologically programmed to want and need their parents' love and attention, leading to a complex, often greedy-seeming desire to remain front and center in the eyes of the people who are literally keeping them alive (that would be you). Even after they no longer need your constant attention, they continue to crave it.

Siblings, of course, are big time competitors. They also want and need you for themselves. So kids continually vie for the biggest prize—you. Your time. Your attention. Your favor. Your love.

Now as you well know, you can give your time, attention, favor, and love to all your children; you don't have to choose just one. But that's not how they see it, especially if you have been stepping into their battles, mediating, laying blame, telling one or the other what to do.

Parents do this all the time.

Leave him alone.

Just let her use it.

She's younger than you.

To parents it seems logical. To children it is anything but that. It's a contest, pure and simple, and you are the grand prize.

To motivate your children to actually work things out for themselves, you need to remove yourself from the equation. This is probably the single most important thing you can do to reduce sibling rivalry. Stepping out of the role of referee leads to a seismic shift: away from you and back to whatever the argument was about to begin with. With parental favor no longer a factor, the steam goes out of many sibling squabbles.

Of course, not all children have the skills they need to negotiate disagreements—skills like talking and listening, compromising and making contracts, managing feelings and letting things go. *The Sibling Survival Guide* will help children acquire these skills. Bear in mind, however, that this is not an easy process. The concepts, while presented with humor, are actually quite sophisticated, requiring new ways of thinking and behaving that need to be practiced over time.

To maximize benefit, read this book with your child or children. Cover just a chapter or two at a time, pausing to do each of the activities as directed. Talk about what your children are learning; connect the concepts to their lives, and encourage them to actually use the skills they are reading about.

It's common for children to express strong, negative feelings about their siblings. While this might be shocking (and painful) to you, it's important to accept a full range of feelings. Understand their fury, or sadness, or jealousy while helping your children translate these feelings into acceptable language. Don't be too quick to offer advice. Instead, provide support for managing strong feelings. When calm, your children will be better able to find their own solutions.

While there should always be a place for talking in your family, tattling is a different story. Telling on siblings for the express purpose of getting them in trouble should not be allowed.

Empathize with your children, without getting involved in or trying to solve their problems. Your goal is not to end any particular struggle but to support your children in using the coping and conflict-resolution skills they are learning.

Have faith in your children's abilities to navigate their own relationships. Describe your family as a unit, placing a premium on helping one another. Model patience, and the acceptance of individual differences. Avoid the urge to compare your children. Strive to be fair. Keep in mind, however, that "fair" is different from equal. Treating each child exactly the same is an unrealistic (and unhelpful) goal.

For some children, conflict with siblings is just the tip of the iceberg. They might have trouble managing all social relationships. Or controlling impulses. Or tolerating strong feelings. Or maybe your family is undergoing changes, with the addition of new family members, or the loss of a family member. If there are special circumstances, or if your child is having trouble more broadly, you may need to use this book in conjunction with therapy. If your children are harming (rather than annoying) one another, or if there is a high level of conflict throughout your family, please seek the assistance of a mental health specialist.

If you grew up with brothers and sisters, you undoubtedly remember what it's like to both love and loathe your siblings. Clearly in your present-day family, you hope for more of the former. You treasure each and every one of your children and want them to recognize the good in one another—to discover that beneath the brother/sister who chews too loud, talks too much, or hogs the TV lies a fellow traveler.

A helpmate. A comrade. A friend.

CHAPTER 1

Brothers and Sisters Can Be Tough

What if tomorrow morning, when you opened your eyes and rolled out of bed, you found out you were getting a new dog?

You'd probably get dressed super-quick. Go to the bathroom and fix your hair.

Brush your teeth. Wash your face. You might even make your own bed.

You would eat your breakfast, take care of your dishes, and put on your shoes, excited to meet your new dog.

Imagine the dog you'd be thinking about, the kind you'd most like to get. Draw or write about it here.

Dogs are fun. They are:

PLAYFUL   FUNNY

ENERGETIC   SOFT

CUDDLY   ENTERTAINING

HELPFUL   Warm

STRONG   BRAVE

Dogs can also be annoying. They:

MAKE A MESS

CHEW STUFF

HAVE TO BE WALKED

HAVE STINKY BREATH

HAVE TO BE BRUSHED

HAVE TO BE FED

But still, the good stuff is better than the bad stuff, and if you were getting a dog, you'd probably feel pretty lucky.

So, pretend you just did.

After you got your new dog, what would you do?

Well, you'd name him (or her).

Name: _____

And then you'd begin to learn about him.

You'd learn how to take care of him, what to feed him, when to walk him.

You'd learn how to play with him, how to groom him, how to pet him.

You'd learn how to sit together, how to wrestle each other, and when to just leave him alone.

There's a lot to learn about dogs, a lot to remember if you want to get along.

This book *is* about brothers and sisters. But in a funny way, thinking about dogs can point you in the right direction when it comes to the people you live with.

Many kids have problems with their siblings. They find that their hackles get raised. That means they get annoyed. A lot.

They feel:

BOTHERED

IRRITATED

ANGRY

RILED, IRKED, VEXED

NETTLED

PEEVED

HOT UNDER THE COLLAR

AGGRAVATED

If you feel this way, you're not alone. Brothers and sisters can be tough. They can also be great, but it's hard to see the great parts with so many bad parts getting in the way. Bad parts like fighting and bossing. Teasing and jealousy. Tattling. Pestering. You get the idea.

Wouldn't it be nice to get rid of those bad parts? To have some sort of handy-dandy super-deluxe brother-sister changing device to take care of the problem?

Unfortunately, there is no such thing. But it turns out you don't need a brother-sister changing device because *you* have the power to change the way things go between you and your siblings. You do.

Not by threatening them or hurting them.

Not by rolling your eyes and wishing they would disappear.

But by focusing on something entirely within your control—you.

You have the power to stop feeling so bothered, and to start having more fun.

You do.

Keep reading and you will learn how.

CHAPTER 2

The Secret to Seeing Differently

There's an expression you may have heard: "Looking at the world through rose-colored glasses."

What do you think that means?

Rose-colored glasses are imaginary. You can't see them or touch them, but they are still quite powerful.

"Rose-colored" glasses make you see things in a happy sort of way. They help you to focus on the good parts of a situation, which makes it easier to deal with the parts that aren't so good.

Actually, there are glasses of all shapes and colors, descriptions and kinds. We all wear these pretend glasses, sometimes without even knowing it. And whether we realize it or not, the glasses "frame" or influence the way that we see.

Here's how it works.

Remember the new dog you got (for pretend) in Chapter 1? If you were excited about that dog, a pair of **Dogs-are-Great** glasses might magically appear!

Dogs-are-Great glasses make everything about your new dog seem fun. The glasses help you feel so good that, even though your puppy nips, jumps, and chews, you don't mind these things.

The glasses help you ignore these small annoyances, to remember that nipping and jumping and chewing are just what puppies do.

But not all kids have Dogs-are-Great glasses—some wear **Keep-Away** frames instead. Keep-Away frames make puppies seem unpredictable, annoying, even scary.

Imagine you have a friend who wears these glasses.

Let's say your friend comes to your house after school one day.

You hop off the bus, run to your house, and toss your backpacks onto the floor. Your puppy runs over and starts wrestling with the backpack straps, pulling and snarling. You see what he's doing (your Dogs-are-Great glasses firmly in place) and think:

> Look at him. He's so silly!

Your friend sees him, too, only he has his Keep-Away glasses on. Your friend thinks:

> He's tearing our backpacks! Make him stop!

You're laughing and looking for a chew toy, trying to distract your puppy. Your friend is snatching the backpacks away, saying "NO" in a loud, angry voice.

What's going on? It's the very same dog, doing the very same thing, but you and your friend are seeing it in totally different ways.

That's because your "glasses" are different.

Your Dogs-are-Great glasses help you see that your dog is just being playful. But your friend's Keep-Away frames make him think your dog is being aggressive.

Same dog. Same situation. Different glasses.

Now you try one.

Take a look at what's happening and see if you can work out what is in the thought bubbles. Pay attention to which glasses each child is wearing.

27

You realize your dog is saying, "Hi!" Your friend is convinced she's about to be bitten. Again, same dog. Same situation. But you're wearing different "glasses," so you're seeing it in entirely different ways.

Which is where brothers and sisters come in.

Many kids have a pair of glasses they wear a lot—the **Siblings-Stink** spectacles (siblings is another word for brothers and sisters, and spectacles is another word for glasses, in case you were wondering about that).

Whenever brothers or sisters do anything, *anything*, these Siblings-Stink frames make it seem like a major offense.

Have you ever noticed that you say and do things to your siblings you would never say or do to your friends? That's because of your glasses.

Most kids wear a different pair when they are with their pals, something like the **No-Big-Deal** frames.

You might wear these, too. No-Big-Deal glasses help kids shrug things off. That's why you are probably more forgiving with your friends, and why you have more fun.

But here's an interesting idea. What if you wore your No-Big-Deal glasses at home, too? Here's what you might see:

The glasses you are wearing determine not only how you see things, but also how you **feel** and what you **do**.

Pretend you were swimming, and your brother or sister jumped into the pool with a gigantic splash.

If you were wearing your Siblings-Stink glasses, you'd feel MAD. You'd think about what a pest your sibling is, and how the water almost got in your eyes. You'd probably yell at them, right? Or maybe splash them, to see how they liked it.

But what if you had your No-Big-Deal glasses on, instead?

That would make things totally different. Your sibling would still do that major jump, and the water would still splash you, almost in the eyes. But it wouldn't matter so much. After all, your eyes are fine. So, you'd laugh and say, "Good one!" and keep on with whatever you were doing.

How you feel and how you act depend on how you see things.

And there's an added bonus. Changing your glasses changes not only your own behavior, but your brother's or sister's behavior, too. It does!

Here's how it works:

→ Your glasses influence how you see things.

→ How you see things influences how you feel.

→ How you feel influences what you do (that's the part about your behavior).

→ What you do influences what your brother or sister does in return (that's the part about their behavior).

So, to work backwards,

→ Your brother or sister will treat you better.

→ Because you have treated them better.

→ Because you are seeing things differently.

→ Because you are wearing the right glasses.

So, to change *their* behavior, change *your* glasses!

Imagine a pair of No-Big-Deal glasses. Draw or write about them here.

Draw your old Siblings-Stink spectacles in the case.

Use your imagination to snap down the lid.

Start getting used to your No-Big-Deal glasses. The more often you wear them, the better things will go.

Whenever your brother or sister is bugging you, check your glasses before you respond. It might be that you are seeing things through your old Siblings-Stink frames.

Put them back in their case. You don't need them anymore.

CHAPTER 3

Reward the Good Stuff

It's important to put away your Siblings-Stink spectacles because all they do is make you angry. And when you are angry, you are more likely to react to the little things your brother or sister does. Reacting means saying or doing the first thing that pops into your head.

Unfortunately, reacting to your brother or sister causes lots of problems. It might feel good, right in the moment, but it doesn't really help.

In fact, it often gets you into trouble. And worst of all, it encourages your sibling to keep bothering you, which is NOT what you want to have happen.

The opposite of reacting is responding.

Responding means that you are staying calm and actually thinking about what to say and do. Staying calm allows you to think clearly, which makes it easier to do the right thing.

But what is the right thing?

The right thing is to act in ways that are decent and kind. And as an added bonus, the right thing is more likely to accomplish your goal: it gets your brother or sister to treat you the way you want to be treated.

So, in addition to being unkind, yelling at your brother or sister isn't the right thing because it doesn't get them to leave you alone.

Telling on your sibling isn't the right thing because they still barge into your room.

Calling your brother or sister a mean name isn't the right thing because it doesn't teach them to share.

None of these are the right thing because they don't get your brother or sister to treat you the way you want to be treated.

So, what should you do, instead?

You have to be clever, and use something called **Learning Theory**, which is a fancy way of talking about how people learn.

People learn by seeing, hearing, and doing. And they learn especially well when they are motivated—when there's some sort of reward attached to what they are learning.

That's actually one of the rules of Learning Theory:

RULE 1: REWARD THE BEHAVIOR YOU ARE TRYING TO TEACH (TO MAKE IT HAPPEN MORE OFTEN)

This isn't nearly as complicated as it sounds. In fact, if you own a dog, you are probably already using Rule 1.

Let's say you want to teach your dog to come.

You call out: "COME!"

Good luck with that! Your dog doesn't speak English. She has no idea what you are saying, so chances are good she'll ignore you.

Next you try smiling, and calling, "COME!" in a

friendly way. Your face and your voice make her think you might want to play, so she comes running, which is exactly what you want her to do.

So, you say "Good girl" and ruffle her neck and play with her a bit. Voila! You are rewarding what she just did. She came when you called. And by smiling at and petting her, you are increasing the chances that she'll do it again.

You can shape your dog's behavior by rewarding her when she does what you want her to do. It's easy.

If only it worked that well with siblings...

Actually, it does work with siblings!

But wait—before you buy a box of brother-size dog biscuits or even think about ruffling your sister's hair, remember that biscuits and head scratching are rewards for dogs, not for brothers and sisters.

You have to be more creative to come up with rewards for your siblings.

So, think about it. What does your brother or sister want?

Unfortunately, unless you have a secret stash of money, you have no way to give them expensive rewards. But that's okay. Because there are plenty of things your siblings want—things that don't cost any money at all.

Think again.

What do your brothers and sisters want from *you*?

Do they want:

To be left alone

To use your stuff

To go first when you are doing something together

To control the TV

To play with you

To sit where they want in the car

To get some help with a chore

To borrow something from you

To have you stop when they say "Stop!"

Write the name of one of your siblings in each of the small rectangles, then use the larger boxes to write what you think that sibling wants from you. What are the things you can do to **reward** that sibling? It's okay if there are boxes left over.

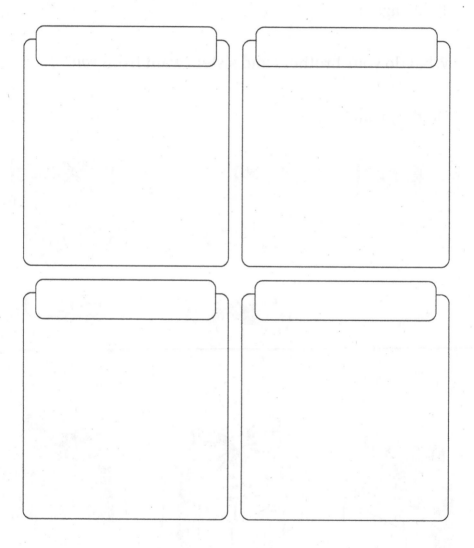

Your siblings will earn these kind gestures (rewards) by doing the things you like.

That's the problem! They never do anything I like.

If you can't think of anything, *anything*, your sibling does right, you must have your Siblings-Stink spectacles on. Take them off and think again.

Do they ever:

* Sit next to you quietly, even if only for a few minutes?
* Leave you alone while you are getting your homework done?
* Let you borrow their things?
* Show you how to do something?
* Crack a joke?
* Play a game with you?
* Keep their feet away from you in the car?

Make a list of the nice things your brother or sister sometimes does—the things you wish they would do more often.

Start paying attention. Notice when your brother or sister plays with you...or lets you use their stuff...or leaves you alone for a while.

These are the things to start **rewarding**.

It all begins with that first rule: reward the good stuff.

These acts of kindness will make the good stuff happen even more.

CHAPTER 4

Don't Take the Bait!

Behavior that gets rewarded increases.

Behavior that doesn't get rewarded fades away.

In other words, if your brother or sister is doing something you don't like, don't reward it.

The best way to avoid rewarding a behavior is to ignore it. Let's call that **Rule 2**.

RULE 2: IGNORE WHAT YOU DON'T LIKE (TO MAKE IT HAPPEN LESS)

No one can deny it. It's hard work to ignore all those pesky, annoying, rude, unfair, awful things your brother or sister does. But ignoring is important AND it works—as long as you're doing it right.

So, take a deep breath...

Make sure you are calm...

And turn your attention to dogs.

Pretend you are sitting at the table eating your favorite sandwich. Your dog comes over and puts her head in your lap. But let's say your family is trying to teach your dog to leave you alone while you are eating, so your dog is not supposed to be at the table.

What should you do?

Well, thinking about Rule 2, you should:

* move your sandwich slowly out of reach
* move your legs slightly to the side, so her head isn't resting comfortably in your lap
* and then keep eating your sandwich.

That's it. You don't have to look at her. You don't have to touch her. You certainly don't have to yell or push her away.

The best thing to do is to ignore her.

That is Rule 2 in action. It is calmly and quietly removing what your dog wants most—your attention, and your sandwich!

Soon your dog will get bored and wander away. Excellent! Now she's doing what you want. So now is the time to reward her.

When you are done with your meal, go find your dog. Play with her. Cuddle her. Tell her she is good.

That wasn't so hard, was it?

You can do it with your siblings, too.

When siblings are bossy or mean or rude, they are, quite possibly, trying to bother you.

When you respond in a bothered way, you are rewarding them by giving them exactly what they want. You are using Rule 1 (reward what you like) to respond to behavior that calls for Rule 2 (ignore what you don't like).

It's time to turn things around.

Imagine you are riding in the car and your brother or sister is clicking their tongue. You can't stand that sound!

But wait. Think about it.

They are clearly bored. Clicking their tongue entertains them and gives them a shot at an even bigger prize—bothering you.

If you insist loudly that they STOP, what's likely to happen? They are going to click even more, right? That's because you have rewarded them. In fact, you have handed over the "bothering you" prize!

So, what could you have done differently?

Well, your brother or sister clicking loudly makes this an excellent time to look out of the window.

Or silently run through your spelling words.

You could imagine a scene from one of your favorite movies.

Or think about what you are going to do when you get home.

In other words, this is the perfect time to ignore your sibling.

Sure, they will keep clicking for a while. But eventually they'll get tired of it, especially if you are ignoring them.

When they stop clicking, you might tell a funny joke. Or let them listen to your music. Or point out an unusual bumper sticker.

You can reward your brother or sister by paying attention to them—once they have stopped making the sound.

Rule 2, ignoring what you don't like, is much harder than Rule 1, rewarding what you do like.

It's tempting to yell at your siblings when they are bothering you. It's like you're a fish, and they have a fishing line. Your sibling is dangling the line in front of you, hoping you will bite the big juicy worm on the end of that line.

Don't bite!

There's a hook in that worm. If you open your mouth, you'll be caught!

So tell yourself, "I'm not going to bite that worm."

Then remember: "I don't like what they are doing, so I'm not going to reward it. I'll ignore it, instead."

And turn your attention away.

You can walk away if you are at home, or pay attention to something different if you are in the car or some other place you cannot leave.

On the next page, draw or write about an indoor activity, an outdoor activity, and an activity you can do in your head while you are busy ignoring your brother or sister.

INDOOR ACTIVITY

OUTDOOR ACTIVITY

AN ACTIVITY TO DO IN YOUR HEAD

Ignoring your sibling using Rule 2 will not make them immediately stop what they are doing. In fact, they might do it even more—trying harder to get your attention. If they continue doing what they were doing, or start in with something even worse, don't panic!

You have to keep using Rule 2 to get it to work. It takes time for your brother or sister to see that bothering you is no longer fun.

So, take a deep breath.

Walk or turn your attention away.

Ignore them.

Don't end up with a mouthful of worm!

CHAPTER 5

Another Way to Ignore—With a Twist

Ignoring is an important skill. Practice it (when your siblings are bothering you) whenever you can. And when you are ready, there's something fancy you can try: **ignoring with a twist**.

Ignoring with a twist is different from regular ignoring. With regular ignoring, you completely tune out your brother or sister, walking away or turning away entirely.

When you ignore with a twist, you continue to interact with your brother or sister while pretending that what they are doing doesn't bother you.

You aren't ignoring them, just their annoying behavior.

There are several ways to do this.

For one thing, you can distract them.

If, for example, your brother or sister is saying your name over and over again, don't tell them to stop—that isn't going to work.

Don't let on that they are driving you crazy (that isn't going to work, either).

Instead, say:

Hey, remember when... (and then describe a funny memory)?!

Or

Hey, have you heard this one? Knock, knock...

Or

Hey, I saw this really cool thing online yesterday. Do you want to see it?

Distraction works especially well with younger kids, but feel free to try it if you have an older sibling, too.

Another version of ignoring with a twist is to agree with what your brother or sister is saying.

Or turn it into a joke.

Here's how that would look:

> *Your sibling: "You stink at baseball."*
> *You: "I know! It's really embarrassing."*

> *Your sibling: "Hey, chipmunk cheeks!"*
> *You:*

Ignoring the behavior, distracting your brother or sister, agreeing with them, or laughing off what they have said—all these tactics work really well. That's partly because this type of ignoring is likely to take your brother or sister by surprise. That's a good thing.

It might make them laugh.

That's a good thing, too.

Ignoring with a twist is a way of shrugging off the annoying part of your sibling's behavior, rather than rewarding it with your attention. And it feels good, too. It might take some practice, and you may need to experiment a bit to see which method works best with your brother or sister, but ignoring with a twist is a good way to change the way things go.

Try it. You'll see!

CHAPTER 6

Dogs Don't Do Dishes

H ave you ever seen:

* A Chow Hound play cello?
* A Great Dane tackle division?
* A Dalmatian do dishes?

Of course not!

That's because no one has taught them, and chances are good no one ever will. In fact, it would be silly to even try.

Why is that?

Well, everyone knows that Chow Hounds don't have finger dexterity (or fingers), Great Danes don't do numbers, and Dalmatians...well, the only way a dog of any kind is going to clean a dish is with his tongue.

When you set out to teach something to a dog, you have to make sure the dog is able to do what you want him to do. Otherwise you'll be wasting your time.

Take making your bed.

What if your dog messes up your bed, lying on it

and rumpling the sheets? It's his fault your bed is all rumpled. He should have to neaten it, right?

Not so fast. Even if you are a great teacher, your dog isn't going to learn to make your bed. He can't. His paws and legs and body don't work that way.

So, what should you do?

Should you mess up *his* bed, to see how he likes it?

Should you yell at him and tell him he's an idiot?

Should you tell your dog he can never come into your room again?

Of course not. Those reactions would be silly.

Your dog isn't messing up your bed on purpose, and he isn't capable of fixing it. He's just being a dog.

It's the same with brothers and sisters.

Sometimes the things that bug you the most aren't done on purpose. And often they aren't things your siblings can change.

Sometimes brothers and sisters do annoying things simply because they are young, or old, or tired, or hungry. Sometimes they do annoying things because it's hard for them to control their bodies or their brains, or because they've had a lousy day.

Chances are good that you are yelling, grumbling, and maybe even seeking revenge for these sorts of things. Things that have very little to do with you, that aren't done on purpose, and that your siblings cannot change.

But how do you know what they can change and what they can't?

You can use your powers of observation to help you sort this out.

When your sibling is doing something that makes you want to scream—or get back at them—ask yourself some questions:

1. Is this something most kids their age do?
2. Is this part of their personality?
3. Do they act this way with other people, too?

If the answer to any of these questions is YES, then trying to get them to change their behavior is like trying to get your dog to make your bed. It isn't going to work.

You'll be happier if you shift your attention to what *you* can do to solve the problem, rather than trying to get them to change.

For example, let's say you have a three-year-old brother who is always grabbing things, including the origami zebra you just spent 15 minutes folding. You tell him to STOP IT!

But wait. Think about it. Your brother is too young to resist touching—it's something all little kids do. And he can't control his hands well enough to touch in a gentler way.

But there's plenty you can do to protect your work. You can fold origami when he's napping. Or make a special animal just for him, to keep him busy while you work on new pieces.

What else do you think you could do?

_____

_____

Or what if you had a sibling in constant motion, always fidgeting, always talking? You are trying to get your homework done. Will growling make that sibling be quiet? Nope.

Your sibling has a brain and body that need to be in motion. They can't stop, even when you are trying to concentrate.

So, what can you do?

Well, maybe you can get earplugs, or go into a different room. Maybe you can work out a private spot to go to, when you need some peace and quiet.

And finally, imagine having a teenage sibling who hogs the bathroom and won't let you in. But you need to get ready for school, too.

It's not worth trying to change this one. Teenagers need privacy, and you've probably noticed that it takes forever for them to be satisfied with how they look.

Maybe you can move your toothbrush to the kitchen, or the downstairs bathroom. Or maybe you can go to the bathroom before your sibling, since you are so much faster.

There are likely to be lots of bothersome things your sibling isn't doing on purpose, things related to their age or personality. Things they do because it's the way their brain and body work.

Some of these things will eventually change (as your sibling gets older), and some never will.

Either way, yelling at your brother or sister isn't going to make a bit of difference. You'll feel better if you can find a way to shrug these things off. Or to solve the problem by doing something different yourself.

Write the name of one of your siblings in each of the rectangles on the next page.

Think about something that bugs you about that sibling. Something that is unlikely to change any time soon.

Make a plan to help yourself feel less annoyed. Something *you* can do.

Maybe you can lock your door to keep a younger sibling from touching your stuff. Or move away from an older sibling when their bad mood is rubbing off on you.

Write your ideas in the boxes under each sibling's name.

Remember:

* You cannot make a Chow Hound play cello.
* You cannot teach a Great Dane division.
* You cannot expect a Dalmatian to wash dishes (except with his tongue).

Instead of trying to get your siblings to do something they cannot do, focus on what *you can do*.

You have the power to help yourself feel better, even if they don't change at all.

CHAPTER 7

Dealing with Feelings

Have you ever noticed that when a dog gets excited, you can see it right there, in her body? Her ears perk up. Her tail waves. She prances from side to side.

See if you can guess what these dogs are feeling from the way their bodies look.

Dogs aren't the only ones who show their feelings with their bodies. People do, too.

See if you can guess what these children are feeling from the way their bodies look.

Sometimes our feelings get into our bodies just a little.

We might feel a twinge of nervousness—just a tiny flutter in our chest.

Or a prick of annoyance—just a small stab of it.

But sometimes our feelings get into our bodies in a big way.

We might feel TOTALLY embarrassed—with bright red cheeks and a pounding heart.

Or BOILING mad—as if our whole body is ready to explode!

If you have a brother or sister, chances are good your feelings get into your body in a big way, at least some of the time.

Think about being with your sibling. Imagine them right there, next to you.

Look at the list below and **circle** the feelings you sometimes feel in a big way when you are with your sibling. **Underline** the feelings you feel in a smaller way. **Cross out** the feelings you don't feel at all.

HAPPY	DISAPPOINTED
ANGRY	CURIOUS
EXCITED	SCARED
JEALOUS	THANKFUL
SURPRISED	WORRIED
RESENTFUL	RELAXED
PROUD	DISGUSTED
ASHAMED	CALM
SAFE	LONELY
FRUSTRATED	LOVING
INTERESTED	WEAK
SAD	GRATEFUL
EAGER	ANNOYED

You probably noticed two kinds of feelings on the list—positive and negative. Some people call these "good" feelings and "bad" feelings, but those terms are misleading.

A positive feeling makes you feel good inside. A negative feeling doesn't. But it isn't "bad" to have negative feelings.

Feelings are signals that your body sends. Negative feelings get you to pay attention to something that isn't going well.

It's important to pay attention to these feeling signals, otherwise they get louder. And when they get too loud, they cause major trouble.

One of the ways to take care of your feelings before they get too loud is by talking to someone and explaining how you feel.

But talking isn't always useful. In fact, sometimes it makes things worse.

That's because there are lots of ways to talk, and only some of them are helpful.

Circle the helpful ways of talking about your feelings. **Cross out** the methods that are not so helpful.

COMPLAINING

BLAMING

USING A REGULAR VOICE

YELLING

CALLING NAMES

NAMING YOUR FEELINGS

EXAGGERATING

SAYING WHAT YOU NEED

It was probably easy to do this exercise. You know it doesn't help to complain, blame, exaggerate, yell, and call names. But chances are good you sometimes do these things anyway.

Why is that?

Well, it can be hard to control yourself when you're experiencing a negative feeling. Especially when that feeling is BIG. Big feelings often lead to unhelpful ways of talking.

That's because when you are feeling something in a big way—especially a negative feeling—the thinking part of your brain shuts down. You stop noticing what the other person is thinking or feeling, and start focusing only on what you want or need.

Big feelings make it hard to remember things like kindness and respect and giving the other person a break because your brain is busy screaming NOOOOOOOO.

So, when you are feeling something in a BIG way, it's important to cool down. Calming down helps to shrink big feelings to a more manageable size, which allows you to think more clearly instead of reacting in a way that's likely to make things worse.

There are several things you can do to cool down.

1. TALK TO YOURSELF (IN POSITIVE WAYS)

We all talk to ourselves, pretty much all the time. This "self-talk" can make us feel better, or it can make us feel worse.

Pretend your brother or sister has just won an award for ice-skating. They talk about their award all the time, and so does everyone else. You feel jealous.

Circle the self-talk strategies that are likely to help you feel a bit better.

Cross out the ones that will only make you feel worse.

"GOOD FOR HER!"

"I HATE IT WHEN SHE BRAGS."

"THAT'S SO COOL!"

"BIG DEAL."

"I CAN'T WAIT TO TELL MIA."

"I NEVER WIN ANYTHING."

It might be tempting to talk to yourself in negative ways, even though you don't mean to. The words simply appear in your mind, and it can be hard to chase them away or keep them from flying out of your mouth.

But there are tricks you can use to talk to yourself in more positive ways.

One is to come up with more helpful thoughts ahead of time.

When a big feeling starts to pull you down, you can tell yourself:

It's not going to help to get all worked up.

I can stay calm.

I'm okay.

Take it easy.

I can handle this.

Practice these helpful kinds of self-talk.

Even if you don't totally believe it, positive self-talk shrinks down big feelings, helping you to feel better inside.

2. BREATHE

Most people aren't aware of their breathing, and that's usually fine.

But when feelings get big, breathing changes. It gets shallow. And fast.

These changes happen automatically, and make you feel as if something is wrong.

So, when you are having a big feeling, pay attention to your breathing:

Work on slowing it down.

Pull the air in through your nose...long and deep.

Count 1... 2... 3... in your head.

Pause, and then breathe out slooowly, 1... 2... 3... 4...

Breathe out through your nose, or part your lips just a little and gently blow out through your mouth.

Then do it all again.

Some kids think breathing is boring. Or that it isn't going to help.

The surprising thing is, it does help. A lot.

Scientists have proven that breathing slowly and deeply is one of the most powerful things people can do to manage strong feelings. You can prove it, too, by practicing this kind of breathing every day.

You might do it just before you start your homework, and again when you are burrowing under your covers to fall asleep at night. The important thing is to find a time every day to practice taking a few of these slow, deep breaths. Pretty soon, they'll come more naturally, and you'll be able to use them to help yourself when a big feeling happens.

3. MOVE

Big feelings have a way of taking up lots of space. When you are SAD or ANGRY or JEALOUS, there isn't much room for clear thinking.

Talking quietly to yourself in a positive way and breathing slowly and deeply will help. But sometimes talking and breathing are hard to do because you are too worked up. You might need to burn off some of your big feeling, to shrink it down to a more manageable size.

When you are trying to shrink a big feeling and you don't want to talk to yourself or breathe deeply, you can move your body instead. Move fast! Do something that gets your muscles working and your heart beating.

ROLL   **CLIMB**

TWIST   POGO

RUN   SWING

SWIM   JUMP

BIKE   DANCE

In the boxes below, draw or write about an indoor activity you can do to burn off a big feeling. Then draw or write about an outdoor activity.

INDOOR ACTIVITY

OUTDOOR ACTIVITY

Be creative. Make sure the activity gets your heart pounding and your muscles working.

When you are feeling a big feeling that you aren't ready to talk about in useful ways—a feeling that seems too big for breathing or positive self-talk—you might not want to do dance moves. Or shoot hoops.

You might be too busy feeling ANGRY or JEALOUS to care about moving around.

Make yourself do it anyway. Just like breathing and positive self-talk, physical activity cools down big feelings and makes you feel better inside.

The point of these three cool-down activities (positive self-talk, breathing, and getting your heart pounding) is not to erase what you are feeling. Your feelings are important, and it's okay that you have them.

The point is to keep your feelings from getting in the way, to shrink them down, so you can deal with what is happening—and how you are feeling about it—in a way that will actually help.

CHAPTER 8

Solving Problems Like People

Bickering with brothers and squabbling with sisters happens for lots of reasons.

Sometimes it's related to not following the rules:

RULE 1: REWARD WHAT YOU LIKE.

RULE 2: IGNORE WHAT YOU DON'T.

Or to big feelings that haven't been taken care of.

But there's another kind of fighting that happens between brothers and sisters, the kind that is all about **power.**

Power fights—like who gets to go first or who gets to decide about something—seem to be about lots of little things. But really, they are about one big thing. Who gets to be **top dog**?

What does that mean?

Well, dogs in the wild live in packs. And in every pack, there's a top dog. The top dog is the strongest, or the oldest, or the cleverest. He's the boss. So he gets what he wants, when he wants it. First. Best. Always.

Except when a new dog comes along. Or if another dog decides he wants to be top dog. Then, watch out! Major FIGHT.

Does any of this sound familiar?

It's what brothers and sisters do. They fight to stay on top. With constant bickering about bigger, better, faster, first.

Fighting to be top dog is a miserable way to live. It takes up lots of time and it keeps you on guard, always having to fight off the competition. That's why people have their own way of living together, a way that is different from dogs.

Here's how it works for people.

1. PEOPLE MAKE COMPROMISES

A compromise is a deal. An agreement in which everyone gets some of what they want, but no one gets all of what they want. Compromises help people live together more peacefully because they are meeting in the middle, or coming up with a creative solution that works for everyone.

There are lots of ways to compromise.

For example, if it's a hot day, and you and your sibling both want the only cherry juice pop, you can compromise by:

* breaking it in half
* doing rock-paper-scissors to decide who gets it
* closing your eyes to choose
* letting your sibling have it, and then you get dibs on the computer
* flipping a coin
* giving the cherry juice pop to your dad (he likes red, too!).

Compromising helps you solve problems as they are happening—not by insisting on having your own way, but by coming up with a creative solution to work things out.

Compromising works best when everyone is calm. So cool down—with the recommendations from earlier chapters—if you need to. Then, follow these steps:

1. Define the problem. Make sure you understand what the argument is about.
2. Focus on the problem without talking in unhelpful ways. No name-calling. No blaming. No teasing. No bullying. Attack the problem, not the other person.

3. Make suggestions about how to solve the problem. Listen to your brother's or sister's ideas, too.

> Kate and I can hang out for 30 minutes, then Keya can join us.

> Keya will leave us alone, and I'll clear the table for her tonight.

> Keya can play for 20 minutes, then she'll leave us alone.

> Keya can play with us, but she'll be the toad and we'll be the wizards.

4. If you say no to someone else's suggestion, come up with an idea of your own.

> I'll start out as a toad, and then you change me into a wizard.

5. Think about solving the problem, not about getting your way.
6. Be willing to agree. It may not be the perfect solution, but at least it will let you move on.
7. Do what you say you will do.

Kids who learn to compromise with their brothers and sisters become talented problem-solvers. They get along better with their siblings. And their friends. And their teachers. And their parents. They feel good about themselves. And have plenty of time for fun.

2. PEOPLE MAKE CONTRACTS

A contract is another kind of agreement. It determines, ahead of time, what everyone is going to do. Contracts are great for problems that happen over and over again. Such as: Who gets to use the bathroom first in the morning? Who gets to play when a guest comes over? Who gets to sit next to Dad at the table?

Contracts often involve compromise, except they don't change every time the problem comes up. They are agreements that everyone sticks to, every time.

Here are the steps for making a contract. You'll notice that they are similar to the steps for creating a compromise.

1. Define the problem.

2. Attack the problem, not the other person.

3. Brainstorm. Make suggestions about how to solve the problem for good. Listen to your brother's and sister's ideas, too.

4. If you say no to an idea, come up with a different one.
5. Be willing to agree on a solution.
6. Write down your agreement.
7. Sign the agreement. This is a promise you are making.
8. Agree to follow the contract for two weeks, even if it doesn't seem to be working. After two weeks, talk about it again, to see if the agreement needs to be changed.

Think of something you and your sibling often argue about. Talk to your brother or sister to create a contract that will help you stop arguing.

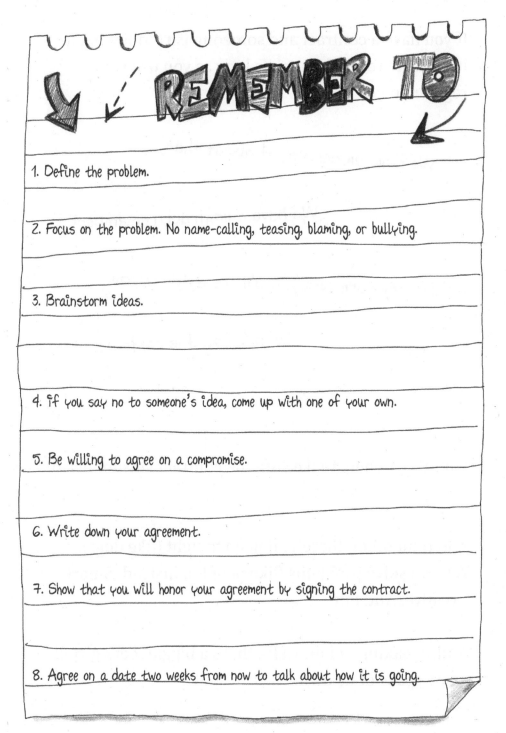

REMEMBER TO

1. Define the problem.

2. Focus on the problem. No name-calling, teasing, blaming, or bullying.

3. Brainstorm ideas.

4. If you say no to someone's idea, come up with one of your own.

5. Be willing to agree on a compromise.

6. Write down your agreement.

7. Show that you will honor your agreement by signing the contract.

8. Agree on a date two weeks from now to talk about how it is going.

If you have a contract and someone isn't following it, it's okay to remind them, as long as you use your regular voice:

We have an agreement about that.

We have a contract, remember?

It's my turn today. You'll get it tomorrow.

Let's follow the contract.

Parents can help make sure the contract gets followed, too.

And remember, there's no need to fight (like dogs). You can solve problems (like people), instead. Smart. Creative. And fair.

And, speaking of fair, well—that's a biggie. Let's give it some space of its own.

CHAPTER 9

Fair and Equal

Y̶ou would never mistake a person for a dog, or a dog for a person. They are two entirely different creatures.

HOW ARE DOGS DIFFERENT FROM PEOPLE?

DOGS	PEOPLE
FOUR LEGS	TWO LEGS
HAIRY	NOT SO HAIRY
TONGUES OFTEN OUT	TONGUES USUALLY IN
WAG TAIL TO SHOW HAPPY	SMILE TO SHOW HAPPY
LEAN OVER TO EAT	SIT UP TO EAT (WELL, MOSTLY)

But there are some ways that dogs and people are the same:

ENJOY TASTY TREATS

LOVE TO PLAY CATCH

HATE TO BE GROOMED (WELL, MOST PEOPLE)

DREAM WHILE ASLEEP

There's another similarity you might not have thought about: dogs and people, especially children, have good "sniffers."

A sniffer is a way of gathering information. For dogs, their sniffer is their nose. Using only its nose, a dog can figure out all sorts of things, such as who has been on a certain street corner or where something that's lost might be found.

Children use their "sniffers" to gather information, too—only human sniffers don't have anything to do with noses, or with smells. What humans, especially children, are able to sniff for is fairness.

Most kids have an amazing ability to "sniff out" differences between the way that they and their siblings are treated. If one child is given something more, or better, or first, children are likely to notice that right away.

It's like that in most families:

Parent: "Let Jesse sit up front this time."
Child: "That's not fair! He sat up front last time!"

Parent: "Let's pick up some corn; it's Ruby's favorite."
Child: "That's not fair! I like broccoli!"

Parent: "Nick, could you help me pick up this mess?"
Child: "That's not fair! Chloe was playing, too!"

When kids say, "That's not fair," it's their sniffer at work. What they are noticing, what they really mean, is: "I'm not getting the same treatment as my brother (or sister)."

And what they really, really mean, deep down (so deep that most kids don't even know they feel this way) is: "My brother (or sister) is getting a better deal. **Our parents must love them more**."

Yikes!

You see, whether you realize it or not, kids who say, "That's not fair!" are competing not only for power, but also for love. That might seem mushy to you, but it's true.

The idea that their parents might love one of their siblings more is so awful that many kids are constantly on the lookout for signs that it's true. They train their sniffers to notice even slight differences in treatment, carefully keeping track of who gets what, and when.

Parents spend lots of time arguing about this, trying to convince their children that everyone is treated the same.

It's exhausting. And the thing is, you don't get treated the same. Things are not exactly equal. They never were, and they never will be. But that has nothing to do with how much you are loved.

There is no limit to the amount of love in a family. There is no way to measure it and make sure it's even. And no need to, either. Your parents love you. All of you. A lot.

Parents do all sorts of things to show how much they love their kids. They:

SAY, "I LOVE YOU"

GIVE YOU HUGS

REMEMBER WHAT'S IMPORTANT TO YOU

DO NICE THINGS FOR YOU

TAKE YOU PLACES

BUY YOU THINGS

GIVE YOU A HOME

KEEP YOU SAFE

FORGIVE YOU

COOK GOOD FOODS

MAKE YOU LAUGH

HELP YOU

TRUST YOU

TUCK YOU IN AT NIGHT

And believe it or not, they try to keep things reasonably fair.

That's important. Parents do try to keep things reasonably fair between their kids. They know that works out best. But reasonably fair is different from exactly equal.

Reasonably fair means giving each child most of what they need and some of what they want. But since your wants and needs are different, sometimes one kid is going to get more, or less. Better, or worse. That's just the way it is.

Your sniffer has been making a major mistake—
spotting things that are **unequal** and calling them
unfair. And that sniffer-mistake is making you
unhappy. But you can re-train your sniffer.

Every time you notice yourself thinking, "That's not
fair!", STOP. Take out the word "fair," and put in the
word "equal." Now you have, "That's not equal." And
chances are good that you are right. Whatever you are
noticing isn't equal.

Next comes the trickier part. Ask yourself if it matters.
Don't jump to what always happens or what never
happens. Pay attention to what is actually happening,
right in that moment. Do you need equal treatment on
that very thing?

For example, pretend your sister just got a new
notebook, and you didn't. Remember, a notebook is
just a notebook. It doesn't mean you are never going
to get a new thing ever again, or that your parents love
her more. Do you need a new notebook? If you don't,
drop it. And if you do, instead of saying, "That's not
fair!" try saying, "My notebook is almost out of pages,
can I have a new one?"

Here's what your parents can do:

Usually when kids say, "That's not fair!" parents get busy trying to convince them it is fair. This is a useless conversation that never turns out well.

Instead, parents can remember, "That's not fair!" really means, "It's not equal," and the chances are good that you are right. Your parents can sympathize with you, or talk to you about what you need. But they should not join you in the comparison.

You are you, and your sister is your sister, and your brother is your brother. You are all different kids, with different wants and different needs.

And your parents love you **all**.

CHAPTER 10

It's Between You and Your Siblings

It takes more than reading to make things different. It takes doing.

If you are truly:

WEARING YOUR NO-BIG-DEAL GLASSES

REWARDING WHAT YOU LIKE AND
IGNORING WHAT YOU DON'T

SHRINKING YOUR FEELINGS WHEN
THEY GET TOO BIG

MAKING COMPROMISES AND
CREATING CONTRACTS

REMEMBERING THAT "FAIR" IS
DIFFERENT FROM "EQUAL"

...you will notice that there is less fighting between you and your siblings. That's great!

But less fighting is different from no fighting. There are surely still squabbles between you.

That's okay. Because believe it or not, you learn important things from struggling with your siblings:

* How to stand up for yourself.
* How to listen to others.
* How to work out your differences.
* How to manage your feelings.
* How to forgive and move on.

If you are like most kids, your brothers and sisters give you plenty of opportunities to practice these skills.

But in many families, there's something that interferes with this practice. It has to do with tug-of-war.

Tug-of-war, as you know, is played with a rope and two teams. Or a rope and two kids. Each child picks up one end of the rope and pulls. And pulls and pulls. Totally determined to win.

Except, it's no fun to endlessly pull on a rope. And it's kind of pointless, anyway. You yank your brother or sister, and still have the same problems you always had. Or you make them fall in the mud.

Big deal—you still have the same problems. That's why you are learning to actually solve these problems.

But stopping these useless tug-of-wars does not happen—cannot happen—if parents get involved as referees.

He wasn't doing anything.

Can't you leave her alone?

Who started it?

When parents say these sorts of things, it's as if they are picking up one end of the rope. If it's your end—YIPPEE—you win! But if it's your brother's or sister's end—THAT STINKS. And that's the problem, because when parents step in on one side or the other, one child is bound to lose.

To a parent, it seems logical:

"SHE'S YOUNGER THAN YOU."

"YOU HAVEN'T USED THAT FOR YEARS."

"YOU CAN HAVE IT BACK LATER."

"WHAT'S THE BIG DEAL?"

But to children, it's horribly unfair. It is also unhelpful. If your parents have been stepping in, you and your siblings might come to expect this. In fact, you might be inviting your parents to join you (in other words, you are tattling). But the more you focus on getting your parents to take sides, the less you get to practice working things out for yourself.

So, it's better for parents not to take sides. Instead, parents can:

* let their children work things out using the strategies in this book
* help their children work things out using the strategies in this book
* separate their children until they are ready to work things out.

117

All three choices work best when they include everyone involved in the fight. There is no need to ask who started it. No need to decide who's at fault.

But what about fights that are serious? Sometimes siblings are truly hurtful to one another, in ways that cause actual harm.

Harmful behavior cannot be allowed. And when parents see it, they need to stop it. Parents can say:

We don't talk to each other that way.

Put that down!

No name-calling.

We don't hit in this family.

No hurting!

Stop!

Often when parents step in to stop the harm, children get busy trying to convince their parents that their brother or sister is to blame:

She grabbed it from me!

He hit me first!

She started it!

He won't leave me alone!

Tug, tug, tug-of-war! Parents should not try to sort this out. It takes two to have a tug-of-war, and whoever is involved is to blame. Instead, your parent can help you and your sibling listen to each other's point of view. They can remind you to compromise. Or to breathe. Or to cool off, so you'll be able to talk more productively.

When parents stop trying to referee sibling battles, siblings stop battling. Or at least stop battling so much. And that's a good thing. Because when siblings aren't battling, they are working things out instead. By talking and listening. Compromising and making contracts. Rope swings and not tug-of-war.

CHAPTER 11

The Good News about Brothers and Sisters

Now you know what you need to know about brothers and sisters, with the exception of one very important thing: brothers and sisters can be great!

Clearing away the major problems makes it easier to see the good things about your siblings. And there are good things. There always are.

Your siblings might make you laugh. Or keep you company. Help you. Or understand you. Teach you things. Or cheer you up when you are sad.

Kids who look for the good things about their brothers and sisters are happier than kids who focus only on the problems. So here are a few final things to think about.

On the next page, write the name of one of your siblings in each of the small rectangles, then use the larger boxes to draw or write about a happy memory you share with that sibling.

Maybe it was the time you made a fort in the family room. Or the time you laughed so hard it felt like you couldn't breathe. Think carefully to come up with a memory you love—one that wouldn't have happened without that brother or sister.

Next, think about one specific thing you like about each brother and sister. Make it something personal. Not "She's good at baseball," but maybe "She's teaching me to slide into home." Think about the things you value about each sibling, the things you would miss if they weren't around.

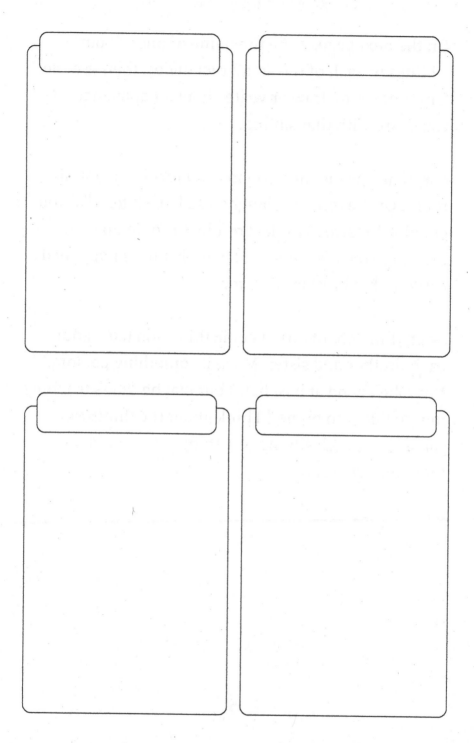

And finally, think about yourself as a sibling. If your brothers and sisters were doing this exercise, what would they say about you? Would they have good memories that you are part of? Would they be able to think of something they appreciate about you?

To have a good brother or sister, you have to BE a good brother or sister.

Write the name of each brother and sister in the boxes on the next page.

Think of something specific you have done to be a good brother or sister to that sibling. Draw or write about it.

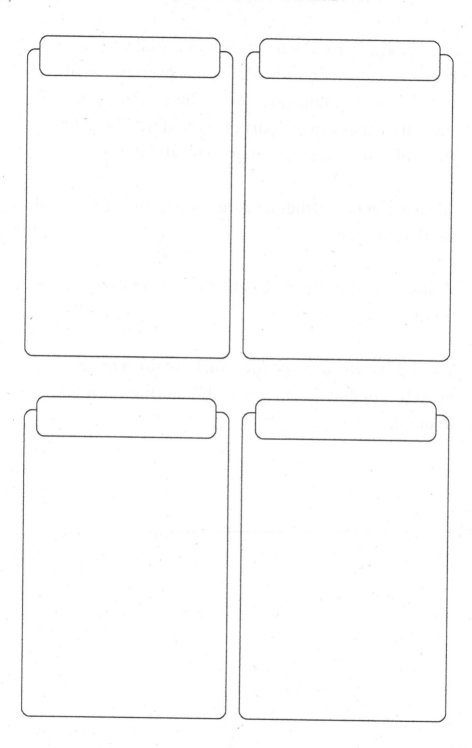

Some kids are surprised to see they can't think of anything positive they have done for their siblings. They've been so focused on what their siblings are or aren't doing that they haven't paid attention to their own behavior at all. That's a problem.

But problems have solutions. And the solution to this one is easy:

Start being a good brother or sister.

Be kind, patient, helpful, funny, forgiving, generous, thoughtful, nice.

Be the brother or sister you want to have. It will help your brothers and sisters be that way, too.

And remember:

REWARD WHAT YOU LIKE
IGNORE WHAT YOU DON'T
TWIST
MANAGE YOUR FEELINGS
COMPROMISE
MAKE CONTRACTS
ENJOY!

There is no one in our lives quite like our brothers and sisters.

And even if you aren't the best of friends, there may come a day when you're glad they're around.

Make that day happen sooner.

You can do it.

You'll be glad you did.